Rivers of Grace:

Poems of Redemption & Restoration

Melanie Houston

ALABASTER BOX
MEDIA GROUP

Book Cover by Lydell Martin

Book Layout by André Hawkins, Kenosis Design Innovations

Editors: Ella Coleman & Amanda Forbes
Photography: Shellee Fisher Photography

Library of Congress Control Number: 2011907294

ISBN-10: 0-9744146-3-8 (pbk)
ISBN-13: 978-0-9744146-3-8 (pbk)

Alabaster Box Media Group, 1750 E. Broad Street, Columbus, OH 43203
www.alabasterboxmedia.com

Contents

Rivers Out of Eden

Your Road to Relationship

About the Author

Products by Alabaster Box Media Group

Dedication and Thanks

This is dedicated to the Holy Spirit, Who breathes words into my spirit so there is life and healing on these pages. My gifts come from Him and I continue to be amazed that He would use me as a vessel. With Christ as the head of my life, I am discovering I can do all things through Him; He strengthens me and transforms my mind.

To my amazing husband, Daniel, who believes in me more than I believe in myself. You are a testimony to waiting on the promises of God. Through this manuscript, I hope you come to understand the journey that brought us together.
I love you from here to Nassau and back again.

To my mother, Roslyn, who did what no one thought possible. You single-handedly raised five children, worked two jobs, kept the house and your sanity. You are the most beautiful and awesome mother a daughter could have. I owe you more than you can imagine.

To Aunt Annie, my sisters (Michele, Theresa, and Teri), brothers (Frank, Andrew), dads (Nick and Andy), and Loretta, your unconditional love has no limits. Thanks for the encouragement.

For all the women in my family – you are the collective sea into which my river flows. I am blessed to be part of a lineage of strong, beautiful women. Thank you for your perseverence and love.

To all my friends, both old and new, this is an answer to prayer.

To all the women and men who tirelessly work the fields of life searching for that great pearl of price, never give up.

With deep and abiding love,

Melanie

Introduction

Rivers of Grace has been an incredible journey in my relationship with family, friends and Christ. It is, to some extent, a journal of my innermost thoughts and simple observances—from driving past a young girl at a bus stop to spending quiet moments in prayer, waiting for God to move in my life. What were, at times, bittersweet paths with missteps and mistakes have turned into fragrant memories of how He brought me through to my purpose. One path to another led me to hope, joy, and times of restoration.

I lend my voice to the forgotten and the overlooked, as well the celebrated and the fortunate. As you turn the pages, know that there is more to our journeys together; this is merely a beginning. I hope you enjoy and deeply reflect after every page.

"The Lord gave the word: Great was the company of those that published it." Psalm 68:11 KJV

Trees Planted Beside the Water

He shall be like a tree planted by the rivers of water that brings forth its fruit in its season, whose leaf also shall not wither; and whatsoever he does shall prosper. Psalm 1:3

The Women in My Family
Every Last One of Them

The women in my family are strong
strong as oak trees in a summer storm
I owe them this poem

The women in my family had to be strong,
Grandma, Tish, Ethel, Midge and Mom
just to name a few
with more kids and less money
than anyone on the block
they fought poverty and despair — and won
We owe them a great deal

The women in my family loved men
who were yet learning to love themselves
and often took more than they gave
they didn't intend to be unintentional
to this day they owe them a debt that can never
be paid and will never be required
love is that forgiving, love is that strong
They owe them respect

The women in my family sacrificed
and pressed for excellence
they taught us to study hard
and made sure we all got an education
no matter the cost
We owe them success in whatever we do

The women in my family stood in the cold and
rain cheering us on at soccer games, track meets
and football games
not forgetting long dance recitals
in auditoriums without air conditioning
they were always there
even when they had to work two jobs
We owe them comfort

The women in my family watched their
happily-ever-after dreams on tv
instead of in real life
after working all day they didn't use the
microwave,
they came home and cooked our meals
Yelling for us to come pick up our things
and take a bath,
they scoured knees and elbows
so they wouldn't be hard and ashy,
and then kissed us to bed
I owe them to be a good mother and wife

The women in my family
made us mad
we wanted independence
they didn't want us to make their same mistakes
We owe them to be wise in all our ways

The women in my family are beautiful
every last one of them
they fill God's rainbow with hues of soft
caramels, chocolates and vanillas
they kiss us and we feel affirmed and loved
We owe them devotion

The women in my family have values
they taught us to behave like we had some sense
and to not show out in public
If we messed up they were the first to defend us
We owe them the right to be
forgiven for their mistakes

The women in my family took us to church
and taught us to pray
they had faith that God would meet their needs
and deliver them, deliver us

and deliver again
We owe them their share of sanctification

The women in my family
made decisions I was afraid to make
they weren't afraid of what people thought
I count them worthy, I call them brave
I owe them honor

Some of the women in my family are now Home
both the young and the old
Missed deeply, they left us a legacy of glory
we are compelled with joy to pass on the stories
of the lives they led
We owe them our past and our present

The women in my family are strong
like oak trees in a summer storm
they live on in life and in memory
yes, the women in my family
every last one of them
are all of that and even more
I owe them peace and a place to lay their heads
I owe them...me

Exiles

As we stood in the sanctuary
The modern-day prophet told us
to close our eyes as he read
from the book of the prophet Ezekiel
He wanted us to visualize
the images and symbols of the passage
Obediently, I closed my eyes

"In the 30th year, in the 4th month, on the 5th day,
while I was among the exiles by the Kebar River
the heavens opened and I saw visions of God. . ."

As he vividly read Ezekiel's four-faced vision
describing the wheel in the middle of the wheel
I stopped at the first verse
The Exiles:
in my mind I could go no further

I rested at the riverbank with the
thousands of Exiles who waited, like me,
for God to move

As powerful as the vision was,
I could not
put the Exiles out of my mind
I identified with them
Exiles from Israel…

I saw millions of my people
waiting on Senegalese
shores for the longest and most
horrific boat ride in history
The passage
The Exiles

From Genesis to genocide
European Jews exiled from France,
Poland, Austria and Germany
to open graves and camps with ovens
there, it would seem, God and the world
turned their heads
Exiles

I saw Rwandan refugees for whom
no one could raise a billion dollars
Floating down contaminated rivers
dismembered and dead
Their bloated passage was to shores of no return
Congress and the world didn't act fast enough
to stop the misery and massacre

I saw Muslims in Kosovo who
ultimately received as much aid, news coverage
and armed forces as this country could muster
With humanitarian relief and military
intervention Congress acted
quickly to prevent another holocaust
Which country is next on the economic agenda?

Looking back again I saw slaves on
Carolina shores
Auction blocks boldly paraded
and tore apart their families
while millionaires were made
and the projects were prepared
Exiled, they waited for God's deliverance
questioning if some civilized person
would show compassion
and end their passage into poverty
before it began

My mind wondered what they
must have felt: shame,
abandonment, rejection,
hostility, fear, anger
or sheer desperation?

Ethnically cleansed
Socially separated
Linguistically lost

I thought I was finished with the vision
of the Exiles, but
appallingly, the revelation of the Exiles remains
relevant today…

I opened my eyes and considered the testimony
of a people exiled to the streets
of New Orleans
a purifying wind and a purifying rain was sent to
show the face and hand of America
with the click of a remote
the world repeatedly saw
the primarily brown and
predominantly impoverished
classified as refugees in and by their own country
Their own government
turned its collective head and emailed itself into
ineptitude, unaccountability and irresponsibility
while deals were made on the golf course
and more than $3 billion a week was spent in Iraq

the most technically advanced country could
not find enough mercy or military might to
transport clean water to a people whose city was
flooded, to those who lived by the lake, the levee,
and clearly, in the wrong zip code…
Surely this was a nightmare from which they
wanted to awaken

Displaced to a dome symbolic of the bottom of an
ancient slave ship,
the Exiles cried out,
"tell everyone they left us here to die!"

New millennium ethnic cleansing and genocide
no longer uses auction blocks and trans Atlantic
trade to separate, destroy and capitalize
It uses natural disasters

Now that strength has rocked Haiti
and all of its inhabitants, will we become
insensitive to the tragic images?
Is there room on our shores for some of them?

Sandy turned out the lights in New York and
New Jersey, leaving their inhabitants numb and
without homes or heat…exiled to city streets,
shelters and schools

It bears repeating — the revelation of the Exiles
remains relevant in the 21st century

We are all, at one time or another, Exiles
Exiled in the heart
and from way down in our souls
that is why we wait
for Righteousness
Holiness
and Peace
That is why we wait for God to move

There is always a river
or some body of water
by which the Exiles must wait

There is a river that flows
from the throne of God
by which we will all one
day be cleansed
and purified
no one is exempt
for we are all, each and every one of us
Exiles

A View from the Other Side

The River of God is like no other
It washes you to places you otherwise
could not go
It heals your heart where wounds are stored
deep and hidden

The River of God is a parable of power and peace,
humility and majesty, mercy and grace
It rushes through you and takes you high
It breathes life and brings life
My God is a River of life
There is not a more serene abode than with Him

He restores life in stagnant places and then
gently laps the shores of your soul saying
Come, follow Me into worship
I have secrets to share and gifts to give
Let Me carry you into My Kingdom

The River of God is His Word
Taking dreams from the pages of your mind
He gives them substance
Just like He did in the Garden

Venture to be rivers
carrying God's Word to the shores of humanity
and His praise to the depths of the sea
a shoreline upon which
the sun lays its head
able to see the power of God dawn
on a new day

Step in…you won't drown

Life with One Woman

When women *touch*
the fragrance of their souls is shared
and you have the option to become part of a
universe

When women *laugh*
it's a soulful sonnet
majestic, moving and immeasurable

When women *kiss*
it is meant to be for a lifetime
and not merely a moment

When women *endure*
it is because they have no choice
giving up only endangers generations to come

When women *cry*
the tears fashion tributaries
that flow into places of restoration

When women *mourn*
there is no solace without healing
no healing without a love to fill the loss

When women *pray*
the Lord hears
and is compelled to respond

When women *praise*
the gates of hell cannot prevail
and somebody is set free

When women *touch*
It is to be held
When women *pray*
it is to hear God

When women *praise*
it is to feel God
When women laugh
It is to express God

When women *love*
it is because women are women
and will always be women
and when women are women and men are men
then all that exists between them becomes all that
is necessary.

If you love a woman you can birth a nation
If you pray with a woman
you can move mountains and lift burdens
If you praise with a woman, cry with a woman,
and endure with a woman
you will understand her strength
and why it is required for you to be a man.

Summer

When winter comes will you be here or should
we even look for you. It could almost cause a woman to
wonder; wonder if knights in shining armor really do exist or
if they are just a fairy tale...

Now we know we will never be rescued from the tops of
castles.
It's time we wrote our own sagas
You know it'll be something about jazz sounds that resonate
in the night, when we stayed up late knowing we had
to get up and go to work. While you kissed us the night
desperately tried to hide us from the morning and we knew
we should've told you to go home.

There are no white horses waiting for us.

The past lives in the sea of forgetfulness
living right is what matters now
Knights will have to cross that sea...
Prepared for battle in the heavens
Sisters of Summer are prophetically prepared
We have read the Book, wept between
the porch and the altar, and have arisen wise.
Somebody has to live the Word.

While we wait for winter and wonder if we'll be warm, we
sit with some jazz sounds that sway in the night and write
our own story about summer and know when it's time
to tell you to go home.

The Women I See

I see women standing at bus stops
waiting for public transportation to take
them to jobs they only tolerate
to insurance companies
that have no blessed assurance
to jobs paying 7 and 8 dollars an hour
so they will be ensured to live at the poverty level

I see women walking children to school
hoping the education they receive will
move them beyond the walls
of the life they now live
intimidated by what is beyond
those double doors
they return home to silence

I see women peering out of windows
wondering if the man is there to disconnect
something
waiting to see what other aspect of their lives
will be cut off next

I see young women – girls actually
strolling babies into a fatherless generation
they can't see the future for the formula
only yesterday they were playing tag

I see women walking campuses like it was
their kingdom
making a way when there was no way
and limited financial aid

I see women lifting up their hands
manicured • wrinkled • holy hands
to bless a God who redeems them daily
and promises never to leave

I see women looking into the eyes
of their men
and wondering
is the color of her skin
the texture of her hair
the curve of her hips
or the shape of her nose
cause for celebration or rejection?

I see women of all shapes and colors
adversity is not particular
white women also
trudge from bus stops
returning home to uncertain
men and uncertain futures

I see red women who want their identity
known and their history remembered
Blending into the landscape of race
no one wants to fully acknowledge their
fight against annihilation

I see yellow women
and I wonder who they think I am

I see old black women — domestics
who still leave affluent suburbs
support hose, canvas bags and city buses
carry them back to where they
have to cook, wash and clean all over again
moving slowly, they wish
Dr. King had been allowed
to live out his Dream

I see corporate women in offices
with state-of-the-art smiles
I pray they are preparing a place
for the sons and daughters
and understand that community
is wherever they corporately exist

I see women in the arms of their men
I watch, hoping these men care and whisper
love poems and sonnets in their ears
holding them tightly against
the night and the odds
saying, "I love you" and meaning it

We all see each
other across bus aisles
at grocery counters and hair salons
brushing by one another during
downtown lunch hours
We find ourselves, our grandmothers,
mothers
and sisters in each other's eyes
and know the art of survival has been passed on.

I see women and my heart is encouraged
On occasion, I find myself able to reach into their
joy as well as their places of praise
As I wait for my promises
I see some women waiting for anything
and anyone

I see women and write
to examine and rejoice in our triumphs and
transformations

Tomorrow when I awake
the first one I will see is
          me
and once again I will see and
celebrate women.

The Bank of America

I lent my back
and a country was built.
In a hot July this nation declared its freedom day
and didn't invite me.
I lent my back
and you used it to step into mighty corporations,
leaving me with crops to share.
I worked — waiting more than 300 years
for 40 acres and mule
you paid me no mind and no interest
Flags fly and firecrackers crack...
I found my own jubilee.

I lent my breasts
nourishing children who would disappointedly
grow to beat, kill, separate and hate.
Now you wonder why violence lives
in my children.
One reaps what one sows,
like father like son.

I lent my hands
hands to serve, to carve out this nation's
capitol and New York City
Hands to sweep, clean, cook and yes, even caress.
I lent my hands.
When I got them back they were dismembered
Disfigured... cut off
I only asked for a hand... not a handout.
The response was to call me lazy.

Explain
How can a people who built pyramids, towers, sphinxes and
cities with little or no technology
be lazy?
lazy people cannot be trusted with a nation
of crops and children.
I asked for a hand, I got shackles in return.

I lent my face so models could fashion
their lips after mine — full with enough passion to
blow you away.
Then I lent my hair so artists could
come to know and create texture.
Imitation *is* the best form of flattery.
I lent my color so you could
measure the sun's bronze impact on skin.
Many want the benefits of my blackness
without paying the price.

I lent my sons for war.
We thought it would make our nation better
to fight for a common cause.
Instead they were sent to the front lines
to buffer the bullets and bombs and then to the
back of the line upon their return home
When will we truly be free?

You tried to take my history
but this generation is ever
reclaiming it, era by era.
You tried to take my men
but they are getting delivered
from self- and system-imposed
prisons.

You tried to steal my vote
But 47 cents is all the **Change** you will get
for the money spent, lies told and ballots blocked
I lent my prince, prophet and priest.
He tried to march us to
harmony and equality.
You silenced him, but not our spirits.
Now you have one of my sons as your president
We have overcome.

You tried to take my homeland,
my first inauguration.
But no one can claim another's Genesis;
liberation is a slow but steady process
People stay but attitudes leave.
My blessing is in My beginning
it cannot be taken away.

In the face of a lie the truth will prevail
and I am the only legitimate lending institution.

Rivers of Living Water

He who believes in Me, as the Scripture has said, out of his heart
will flow rivers of living water. John 7:38

Promised Land Promises
(The Eyes in the Wilderness Tour)

Freedom comes in so many ways
and I think people should see this by now
It raises so many questions:
questions about poverty, famine and hunger
and violence we can't seem to purge
from the faces
of our television sets or our children.
Why is it so hard for this nation to travail
and birth a new child that understands
nothing sacred arises from hatred?
It's as though we are unaware that the children are waiting
for us
Waiting for our prayers...their destinies

The remnant, the "called out," should realize it is they who
will lead the people into the Promised Land
You see, Moses started it
Caleb crossed it
then Martin saw the glory of it,
so we ought to finish it.
Understand, it's less about the color of your skin
and more about being blessed enough to open the door for
someone else.
Freedom comes in so many ways.

This land that we live in holds the blood
of our ancestors.
Irrigated by the sweat of their brow,
it will cry out to us until we pass this vast darkness
and find the light of the Son.
It's a burden light enough to bear
and a dream that has been deferred
We have one last river to cross on this tour
and then we shall see the day.

The activists used to say free your mind
and everything else will follow
My Lord says, "Know the Truth and the Truth shall make
you free"
But some say He was just a man...
Yet, I look for a man
One who is graced to stand in the gap and
without hesitation make up the hedge.
I've been inside Isaiah, and journeyed Jeremiah,
for days way down in Daniel
and I am still found wanting.

I look for a man to lead us into the
Promised Land.
The children are waiting for us
What can we do to redeem the time?

Freedom certainly comes in many ways,
and while standing on this
monumental mountain,
I look for a man to lead
my people and me into the Promised Land.
Looking through the mist of
opportunities, I venture to see the
Promise and prophesy.
Although it's hard to understand why
freedom's sunset is fast disappearing and why we are still
walking through the valley of
the shadow, I have to believe
in those brave enough to repair the breach and
find my own brick.
We are obligated by the Cross to
bind shadows that hide
our liberation and mock our liberality.

So I pray for the fullness of this season while I look for this
man to let love liberate us into the Promise.

I pray that we as a people will get there.

A Remnant Woman Revisited
From Isaiah 54

Woman put down those blues and shout
In your spiritual travail as you laid before the Lord
Interceding
the intercession
and entering in His presence,
you birthed many children
causing His glory and power to show forth

Prepare yourself, open wide the
windows of your mind
Your God is about to do a new thing in you
The dream that is within you, and the seed you will one day
bear
are going to reclaim stolen lands and destinies
It shall be a revolution with
restitution and restoration

With blessed boldness speak forth His praises
when you see and feel the hand of God upon you
you will forget the past
forgiven by
forgetting
forever and forever

He has been to you as a husband
You are birthed and born again for His purpose
He saw the past rejections and the pain of losing who you
thought you were
His mercy is ever upon you and He does not forsake His
daughters
He has a love for you that burns like a ruby
blinding
blazing
and ever blessing
And even if He is silent, His promises are sure
While mountains melt and hills hide,

compassion and peace
are the covenants claimed for a remnant woman.

Dismiss the doubts—release the potential
He is making you beautiful again by
Showering you with precious stones and valuable gems
This is your foundation
Everything around you will be made beautiful in its own
season
shimmering outside
shining inside and
supremely sovereign
Selah. . .(pause and reflect)

Your children will be full of wisdom
and know who they are
teaching and
reaching them
restoring the breach in them

Come to a place where there is no need
to take your fears
the oppressor and those who tried to destroy you
are removed and bound from further subversion
The pain they created was your purification process
With you they will find and make peace
No weapon
No weapon formed
No weapon formed against you
No weapon formed against you will prosper

Be secure • Be vindicated • Be triumphant
Put down the blues
and in their place find a garment of praise
Sing a fruitful song in a barren land
Sing loud and strong
You have every right
You have His righteousness
You have some heritage to keep

Selah

Full

Faith full God
Lets us fall in love
    over and over
looking over our shoulders
overtaken by His grace
we are grateful for a covenant full
            of blessings
        exceeding
        abundantly
        above
        all we
asked or imagined

    this is how it works

filled with faith
and a mercy full God

care full not to forget
to say

thank you

for the wonder full
beauty full gifts

Who Am I?

When I slip behind the veil I know You are real. With a
motion of Your finger I follow.
There I find the mystery of Your love waiting for me and I
glimpse into where You live.
It is where You've been waiting for me all day.
It is there I feel grace and mercy in waves and I
strain to hear Your voice.

Not mere emotion, my tears have a purpose.
As they fall they water a destiny emerging toward fulfillment
Somewhere a prayer is being answered; a child is rescued;
a family finds refuge, and I am resurrected.

No longer silenced by the fear of an unseen enemy I cry out
long and loud. No one to hear but You.
That is enough.

Every thought is emptied in Your presence
I can hide nothing from You
You know my every need and my thoughts
from afar off.

Who am I that You are mindful of me, both the
psalmist and I ask?
Who am I that You would use my words
to heal the generations?
Who am I that You call me mighty and cause
me to walk in a wealthy place?
Who am I that You give me the mind of Christ,
the wisdom of a multitude
and a voice that soothes the nations?
From You I have the tongue of the learned, the
wings of a dove, prayers that move mountains,
and the favor that only a daughter can obtain
from her Father. Who am I?

Who am I? What awesome and mighty things
You have called me to. I am both honored and
humbled. How am I to walk, to what people am
I to speak? Where do I go and whom do I say
sent me? To what work do I put my hands?

Sanctify me again and again; renew me and
cleanse me in Your righteousness. Make me
Your eternal Excellency. Clothe me in Your
grace and humility, anoint my head and my lips
with a word from Your throne. Veil me in virtue
so deep that my desires become one with Yours.

Don't You know, without You I am nothing?
Do you realize how much I need You?
I cannot live without Your breath within, Your
hands beneath, Your eyes to watch, Your words
to teach and the hem of Your garment to grab.

When I have no one else, I have You. Even when
You remain silent and as hard as I try I cannot
hear You, You exist in that silence and watch me
grow.

You are my prosperity, You are my provision and You are
my peace. You are my praise. You are my praise. You are the
only faith I have ever needed.

I love You. I love You. I love You. I love You. I love You.
I cannot live without You.

The thought of life without You brings desperate thoughts;
please don't take Your Holy Spirit from me. When I am with
You I am with eternity.

You take my breath away. Feed me until I am
filled with Your presence and let me drink from the living
waters that flow past Your throne.

I am Yours.

I will bear the ridicule and rejection as I pass through the narrow gate. It is a small price for being wrapped in Your majesty and caught up in Your glory. Until the day I find myself escorted to Your kingdom, I am eternally yours.

Where do I go from here?

What paths do I take?

How will I know when I arrive?

With a motion of Your finger I follow and for tonight, that is enough.

Fragments

Fragments of hurried conversations
I do most of the talking
You listen
Not enough…just not enough

Needing to push away the world's voice
and all that it calls out to me
This piece of paper becomes the obeisance
I owe — my worship, my prayer

That which I spend most of my time on
becomes what I worship
fleeing the freedom of You
I disappoint myself
Where did You go and why did I leave?

Now that I'm here I don't want to leave
I look up and try to kiss Your face
with my worship
will psalms ever flow from these fingers?

Patiently
You use the elementary elements of
my emotions to draw me back to
Your embrace. The wisdom and
passion of this love finds
and calms me

Then You remind me
of a Grace that is sufficient
A Word that never changes
Strength made perfect by weakness
a Kingdom without end
a Blood that redeems
Stripes that heal
a Name above all names

An Infant King
a Carpenter's Son
a Priest who became His own sacrifice
the Lamb of God

You multiply by dividing
Add by subtracting
Live again by dying
Rise after being buried
Justify by faith
Save by grace
Call many but choose few
Forgive when I ask
and live in my praise

You open heaven's windows
Magnify Your Word
Renew strength
Order footsteps
Light the way
Conquer death
Open prison doors
Set captives free
Lift burdens
Destroy yokes
Give beauty for ashes

and...
you know my every thought

Even with mere fragments
I can live again.

Talk with God During Worship

Tell the people of My great love for them. Tell them that I died so that they would live with Me forever. There are places of paradise already prepared for those who accept Me, those who are willing to go beyond the veil of their flesh and drink from Me. I am the River of Life that fills the thirsty soul. When they come to Me, they will find rest from all that concerns them and makes them weary. They will find peace and comfort. I am that place, that thing they have been seeking, but have been unable to find. I am the River that flows from the throne of God in heaven. I am things too lofty and too high for them to even imagine. I am their beginning and their end, their first and their last, their soon coming King. I am Christ, the Anointed Son of God, who now sits on the throne. With love, I daily make intercession on the behalf of My sons and daughters, My brothers and sisters. I AM that I AM.

Break forth into a spirit of praise and you will find Me there. Always remember that I dwell in the midst of your praise. Praise pleases Me and is pleasant to My ear. There you will always find Me. I am never lost when praise takes place. My Holy Spirit makes His way to you, to answer prayer and leave more of His Spirit. This I give to release the people from the many fears and burdens they have carried for years. Tell them of a place of paradise that exists. It is a place that exists for My worshippers—those who worship Me in spirit and in truth.

This is a true and just saying received from heaven. I have sealed it by My Spirit.

Memorial Stones

Then you shall answer them that the waters of the Jordan were cut off before the ark of the covenant of the LORD; when it crossed over the Jordan, the waters of the Jordan were cut off. And these stones shall be for a memorial to the children of Israel forever.
Joshua 4:7

An Alabaster Box

Every time I see a funeral procession
I wonder for whom it is held
You can usually count on the fact that it is
someone who was loved;
it used to be that you could speculate
that most funerals were for those in their
twilight years
ready to go to a better place.
But somebody's child died today.

Now when I see a funeral procession
I wonder if it is a young black boy —
another soul slain;
another life counted worthless. . .
I see mourners in long black cars, headlights
glaring and faces wrought with grief;
Our graveyards are full to capacity
They have to be.

Christ said let the dead bury the dead
today the young bury the young
Could you endure if you had to
bury your brother riddled with
bullets at the age of 13?
could you bear pushing a coffin
into a hearse of an 18-year old
college-bound athlete
a victim of a drive-by shooting?
we bury the innocent
we bury our dreams
fatally, we bury our future
and today somebody's child died
Another unacceptable sacrifice.

No one addresses the fact that
these kids really don't
love themselves. Unlike Melchisedek
the bronze high priest
they don't know their beginning of days
they only know the ending of life

I cry for kids I don't know
I read about them in weekly magazines
and listen to their sad stories
on public radio
they are somebody's child
someone's brother
someone's grandson
(and why is it the bullets are primarily catching
our young men?)
in a way I think the kids today are
brave — I couldn't bury my friends
as frequently as they are required.

If we collected all the tears of
the mourners: tears of fiancés left
not at the altar, but at city morgues;
all the tears of the fathers and grandfathers
the mothers, sisters, grandmothers
classmates, and little kids who live
in housing projects
there would be no drought in Africa
Surely we would have a rainforest.

Put my tears in an alabaster box
and pour them out into the
streets as a sin offering for
the transgressions of my people

for all their anger and despair;
for all the violence that has no
where to go but into the heads and
chests of our young princes;
for all their lack of knowledge of
who they are, and
for all their self-hatred.

Perhaps then I could dry
my eyes one last time
saving my tears for those who
die quiet and full.

The Grand Cosmos of the Sistahood
(@ Debora)

Graced for the journey
One would think you are an angel
in a black woman's body
try to define the grand cosmos of sistahood
and i find you in it
But.for.real.
You are

an angel
Can't nobody tell me otherwise
Knowing you is like knowing power
Like apprehending a ballet and a
symphony in your mind
witnessing grace under fire
and finding yourself amazed
…and finding yourself
Overcoming all that tries to stand against you
You are what everyone woman needs
a sistafriend
you have always had my back

Selah on that

2 Chronicles 20: when we don't know what to do
our eyes are on Him

we are graced for the journey
more than conquerors
overtaken by blessings
and daily loaded with benefits

i.want.you.to.always.remember
the battle is not yours
it belongs to Him
praise stills the enemy

and brings the presence
of a holy God

i.need.you.to.always.know
that i love you like a sista
nothing can separate us from the
love of Christ

you are my since-4th-grade-friend
nothing can separate us
not a thang

Selah, my sista
Selah

Life in One Night
A short story

They sat as black women have always done — on the porch, late into the evening.

They were single women, married women, women bearing children, and women in anticipation. Born into different circumstances, they had the consummate knack of being comfortable with one another, even if for the first time. They sat as if they had sat a hundred times before.

They spoke of men, and the unspoken wars raged against the people. Wars raged against the men and the children. Wars raged against them. They were women at universities, hospitals, and corporations. Each one was separate, but equal — equally misunderstood and equally existing. Each was never separate from the other, bound together by a turbulent history, soft songs, and spirituals whispered in the night. They would continue this way along their journeys to eternity.

"Before I leave here, I want to organize one day when all black people call off from work…just one," proposed the college professor.

Thoughts circled in the night air.

"Garbage wouldn't get collected."

"There wouldn't be anyone at the hospitals."

"Hmmph…No one to teach our children?"

"No hotel desk clerks? And, what about the banks and car assembly plants?"

"Girl, what about law firms and television stations? No one would be there."

Amused, they all cited areas where their people made contributions without always receiving recognition.

"Cities would have to shut down. The whole country would come to a halt...yeah..."

They wanted to stop everything for just one day, so everyone would realize that the majority of them were not on welfare.

They spoke of men — husbands, sons, fiancés, fathers and brothers.

"I'm sorry, but they are all stupid. They say stupid things, do stupid things." The women laughed, knowing their classification of men was dubious and couldn't be fairly applied to all. "They are stupid."

"You have to work with them. Poor things."

Everyone contributed. Everyone sighed. The poet wondered what that meant for single women like her with expectations. The one about to marry was satisfied her man did not fall in that category.

Each of the women comprehended the price. It was true that men owned some degree of inherent insensitivity, but deep inside the women knew they would rather love them and be loved, than to face a future detached from the links to their children and their destinies. The women were not that unreasonable. They appreciated the wisdom, the creativity, the dedication, and the pursuit of a better life that came from their men. They looked to their strength.

To be honest, the women knew that they did not want to dance alone. They recalled the past, were thankful for the present, and dreamed of future loves. It made absolutely no sense to abandon what was theirs. They would continue to accommodate the flaws in their men's characters, just as the men acquiesced to theirs. They needed their devotion.

As the sun began to lay its head on the horizon, the women concluded that the treatment given to the Haitians would never be offered to Europeans or Asians. "It's just because they're black and you know it. If it were anybody else they would let them in," they agreed.

"It's only because we don't have any collective power as a people that they can get away with it," declared the one with child. From the South, she knew all too well about collective action. "If I had the money, I would buy all of them a plane ticket. Then there would be nothing they could do. Once they hit the airport they have to give them political asylum."

She was a firm believer that black people, boats, and water were not a good combination. History had not been kind to her people in that way, a well-documented fact. The greatest redemption they had found was in the waters of baptism.

Without uttering a word they all agreed, wishing they had the money to show the world they were as connected to the boat people as the people in their own immediate lives. Others needed to comprehend that whatever was happening to the Haitians affected their people as well, in places that cannot always be seen. They sat silently. They sat feeling helpless.

"Sending in the military isn't a good idea either," said the one about to be married, conscious of the fact that her current state of bliss did not negate her people's suffering. Her bliss was not to last. The man of her dreams was merely acting his way into her heart. In time, God would give her another who walked with integrity and honor.

They were all troubled about the military going to small black countries with big guns and big planes. They understood the definitions of colonialism and imperialism. All black people should learn those definitions.

Hugging her knees, the poet reminded them of their purpose for being conveyed on wooden boats with metal chains: to serve as a labor force. "It was never intended for us to be sitting here free, educated and building companies. We were never supposed to achieve. If labor were needed now, the Haitians would be received with welcome arms."

Flowers closed and crickets sang. They appreciated the sounds and smell of summer. They counted their blessings.

"If I had the money, I'd send 'em all a plane ticket," the one from the South repeated softly, caressing the child within.

The woman from the islands sat and listened, sharing her wisdom sparingly. While she was overjoyed for the woman with child, she silently recalled the death of one of her sons. Nevertheless, as women were accustomed to doing, she was there to bring gifts of celebration for the new life that was to be born. They were all there to celebrate the new life about to emerge into a society filled with opportunities and contradictions. Angelica would be her name.

As they thought of the plight of the Haitians, no one could have told them that years later a great shaking would take place and tear the diminutive island apart, leaving the children as orphans and the people homeless, without food, shelter or water.

The women felt safe in that neighborhood on a night not touched by calamity. No helicopters circled. A missing child returned home safely; by now he was in bed. Acknowledging their security and looking out into the night, they offered up hushed prayers for nameless victims.

The night moved on. They spoke of racism and relocation.

"It doesn't matter where you go, it's everywhere. Nothing will ever change," claimed the one from the South.

Again silence. The rules were violated daily, without

understanding that it was proper to apply justice. Unfortunately, they were put in positions of having to remind those in power of that fact. The result: job evaluations that described them as not being team players, as aggressive, or having attitudes. The response: documentaries on racism that questioned and explored its existence, as if that was supposed to make someone, anyone, feel better.

Parallel to the women in each of their pasts, they also had boundaries. Daily they awakened praying that no one would push them to their respective limits, allowing them to return home sane. Taking Bibles and sandwiches to lunch, they believed the words they read. Those words soothed them until five o'clock, and then motivated them to triumphantly return the next day. Unbeknownst to them at that very moment God was building a foundation and doing a work in them. His strength was being perfected in their weakness. In the course of their trials, He was causing them to be lights in dark places, the salt of the earth that would make others thirst for rivers of living water. Within years, God breathed on each of their lives and caused divine destinies to be revealed. They would emerge as the employers rather than the employees, kingdom builders, and agents of change. God had already breathed on the one from the South; her life was forever changing as the child inside grew.

Like their ancestors, the women would teach their sons and daughters how to survive in concrete jungles topped with glass ceilings by using the resources of heaven and earth. This would become their testimony and legacy.

With dogs barking and children darting home on bikes, the women left the porch to clean up; to wrap leftovers in foil for husbands and kids and to tear down paper streamers. Quietly, they left one another to continue journeys that began long before they met. Someday soon they would sit on other moonlit porches with different women just like themselves, resurrecting their strength and wisdom to pass on to other generations for another day, another decade, and another century. The pages would gently turn in each of their lives, volumes to be lived and more dark nights to wrap and kiss blackness within beautiful blackness.

Perfume Ladies

Have you noticed?
The perfume ladies at the mall
only watch as I saunter by
They rarely ask me to try a sample
Their make up tightly applied
lips tightly shut,
they glare, not smile as I approach
They must not see me or want to share
their merchandise
Perhaps there simply isn't enough perfume to go around…
perhaps

I'd rather be a fragrance
in the temple of the Lord
Like Esther I will bathe
until my scent reaches His holy throne

No need for perfume ladies
whose fragrance dies at day's end
I'll lift my hands, my voice and prayers
and ascend like the gardenia I am to the
Hill of the Lord

Assassination

I remember where I was when he died
I laid sprawled under my sister's crib, listening to the radio.
I was to turn 10 four days later and that evening I learned a
new word.
The announcer spoke of a man who was assassinated.
It was the first time I heard that word.
I wondered who this man was
they kept referring to over and over.
Assassinate
I quickly learned that it was a death;
A violent death.
I would hear it again and again.
Assassinate
Assassinator
Assassination
We are a nation that assassinates its leaders
We are an AssassiNation

In my youth as the night continued,
I grew older.
I realized my people had lost an important part
of their struggle.
He restored dignity to our daily existence.
He made certain men listen so hard
they worried that the rest of the country
would awaken from a deep slumbering trust of
a system that sent teenage boys to a war
that was not ours,
on a piece of ground we did not own.

I read his "I Have a Dream" speech
in *Jet* magazine.
Keeping it for several days, I read it
over and over again.
I remember the picture of the crowd that gathered
themselves
and their struggles from distant places.

Today we gather from distant places
wanting our records of "the million"
to be recorded in history.
We come making promises
becoming Promise Keepers;
We come marching men – seeking atonement
that was already given at Calvary
Christ's voluntary assassination paved the way
and removed the shame of not taking responsibility for the
women and the children.
We come as women willing to share our pasts
and learning to love again,
promising that if we have to do it by ourselves
we will take back our children and our communities.

I learned more about him in death
than during his life. Visiting his memorial
there is something eerie, yet peaceful that takes
place within you.
You sense that an enormous
mantle must now rest with someone.
We must pray for the life of anyone who has the
courage to pick it up and wear it.

Let us, therefore, pray
against the spirit of racism, hate and violence
that runs throughout this nation.
Pray that no more bombs kill innocent lives
for causes that don't advance and most don't understand.
Pray that our children lay down their weapons
and study war no more.
Pray that we take the time to hug and love our children,
teaching them acceptance
no matter who they are, what they look like
or where they come from

Pray that places of worship burn
with the fire of the
Holy Spirit and not gasoline.
Pray that our leaders live according to godly principles and
not greed.
Pray for God's mercy upon us as a people.
Pray for peace, purity, and the prophets
who are
and who are to come.

Extraordinary Wind

Carry me away with You
Carry me away to a place high above the earth
Where I exist in an eternal embrace

I want to go where You go, to deep places of love and where
the mysteries of Your kingdom exist.
I want to see inside the place where You abide, where You
live and reign in eternity
Tonight I want to go where You go

If not tonight, can You take me with You the next time?

Oh, how much I need you…
Hold me and then let's dance

There has to be an extraordinary wind that carries only You

I want to soar on it with You …just us…feel You hold my
hand and pull me close to You
Discover something You just recently created
Sit with You by a gentle stream and share my
deepest thoughts
Let you brush away my fears and reassure me that, yes, we
can come back again.

Is this water shallow enough?
You know I can't swim.
Deep enough for you to learn how.

How high is that mountain?
You know I don't like heights.
Just high enough for you to stretch your arms and fly over it.

Will the wind blow against me like at home where it can be
so cold?
Just enough to push you closer to Me.

I don't want to go back. Can't we stay a little longer?
I have a people waiting for you to touch with the words you write; to speak a word of deliverance and to let them know that My love awaits them and that I died for their eternal destiny with Me. Tell them I am real and the only God they will ever need. There will be plenty of time to come back here.

When?
When you seek Me and search for Me with all of your heart. I'll call you and you'll know it's Me.

You won't forget, will You?
How can I ever forget about you? Remember, I am Jehovah Shammah, the One who restores, Who never leaves, the ever-present God. No. I won't forget you.

Is it time to go? Will I be able to find my way
back here again?
Yes, but you can stay as long as you like in My heart. My Word will always guide you back to Me. With it, you can never get lost.

Can we have one more dance?
The pleasure is all Mine.

Did I tell You that I love You?
I love you, too.

Places of Pride, Pain and the Press

Tonight I met a woman who I knew before,
but now I know again
She knows many things
She knows of separation and beyond
and has a song of the night, a song that only
women who have suffered loss can sing
She is this poem woven in a widow's garment
She has become a spirit of praise,
exchanged for heaviness
I pray that what she hears from my spirit will
mend another part of her heart

As women, we should listen to each other
especially when night falls,
It is a time set aside for quiet healing
Angels listen
and carry our prayers back to the
Throne of Intercession
In telling our stories we find
we have not been abandoned
and discover our promises in the days ahead

So . . . we picked up where we had both left off
Places of pain, pride and the press
Involuntary journeys taken so that others may
heal and be made whole
Together we found we had to leave pieces of pride behind in
our separate gardens
to gain entrance into the press
She has lived at Gethsemane's gates long enough
Gethsemane is that place where pride dies as you drink
from your cup
The anointing costs – it is a price paid

I can't imagine her pain
I don't want to imagine her pain, although mine has been
just as real

She buried her memories in consecrated ground
I buried mine in a box, pushed back in a closet
With three children, she lives down the street
She works to show her strength,
sustain her house
and restore most of her dignity
Her daughters will be strong,
Her son a gentle, but mighty man

Tonight when I talked to God I found her tears on my cheeks
and her smile in my heart
I learned something about myself
I asked for forgiveness for the sin of pride
and not wanting to let go of my flesh

As I waited for my new day and the fresh mercies
He promised
I found His faithfulness great
and mine increasing

In these involuntary journeys and during times of
intercession
I know I will find other women's tears
they are precious offerings
Saved by our Savior
He reserves them and pours them out for healing streams
and living waters in our deserts
they never run dry

Tonight when I talked to God
I talked about her
and places of pain, pride and the press

Pressed into Eternity

Another night in Your presence
I wrap myself in Your arms and speak Your Word out loud
When I'm with You nothing else matters
I can raise my hands to Your face and kiss You in worship

Here lies peace as I bow my head
Here falls joy as I sing Your praise
Here I understand how I have missed You
by not spending time
Why did I stay away so long?
What was I thinking?
Yielded, my intercession reaches Your throne

Not wanting to leave I beg time to stand still
and suspend me in mid air
like a child arching through
the wind on the backyard swing,
I press my face into eternity

In this quiet Your faithfulness is greater
and my transgressions fall away
Things hoped for don't seem so out of reach
Promises are kept, miracles await
The alabaster box of my heart breaks open
This time You anoint me for another journey
another season
holding on, I don't want to leave
turning away, I blow one last kiss

Rivers Out of Eden

Now a river went out of Eden to water the garden, and from there it parted and became four riverheads. Genesis 2:10

Silent Journey
(From Ethiopia to Israel)

A stranger, an Outsider I'm called
But I just want to come home
My journey began when Egypt was strong
And Ethiopia had food to feed us
Hundreds of miles separate me
from the place of praise
Mt. Zion: the holy hill where my God dwells
Israel

I have walked the desert with my staff
And crossed borders with my bags
I go silently, saving precious breath
Saving this worship for Zion

Some went Home by another road
Through the gates of glory
Perishing by the way, their strength slipped
from lack of grain and grace
to finish the journey
Now their spirits await me on the mountain
They finally found the place where our God dwells

When I come Home to Zion I will have
enough food for my children
A place to lay their heads
A place to stretch forth our hands
And a place for a praise to go throughout
the ends of the earth
all the way from Zion

Thoughts on Revolutions

Upside down
The world is up
Side
      Down
The people want more freedom

We pay more for gas and food
Freedom is expensive
Some have.are.will.died.dying.die
Rising up in a square
Notice: squares are where everything takes place
Dynasties, despots and demigods flee after
                       stubborn resistance
Pilfering their wealth on helicopters or
private jets,
they relocate to remote islands and cavernous mountains

Mycousinwenttowar…hecameback…a blessing for
generations of families
He now prays for others' sons.daughters.husbands.wives.
fathers.mothers.brothers.sisters

Nightly news and YouTube provides a front row seat of each
revolution…fact is, gil scott told us
               the revolution first takes place in the mind and
it cannot be televised. The revolution will not be televised.
willnotbetelevised.

Ancestors' Honor
(In Memory of Helen & Vernencia)

Washed in water

Clean

New memories begin to dance with me
And I see the passage
Quietly, yet assuredly I pick my way down
paved streets
carefully holding my own alabaster box
anticipating the chance to share this anointing

tall buildings try to mock me
calling out their strength and importance
corporate ladders within don't fit anymore
I already shattered all the ceilings
      if you ask the walls
      they might remember me
            oh yes, she was strong
      they would say

tossing aside the calls to come back in
      I see it was never meant to be secure
           or safe

Inside this covenant of marriage we walk an uncharted path
To peaceful streams and gentler conversations

Our avenues are hushed but filled
with the pride our ancestors always willed
we would have

Heads no longer bowed down
We sense their approval
They can rest now
We have a purpose and an abundant harvest.

Single

My soul is a single candle that burns
in a dark room on a table
sometimes by one bed
one single source of light
in a life that has found peace

My soul can be a single tear that falls
from the face of a child who has lost
her family

Tonight my soul is single

My soul is a single mother
with one job
in a sea of many, she lives from one
day to the next with
the hope of redemption

My soul is a single prayer
whispered
on a night while the moon shines down
it could be anyone's prayer
of faith and thanksgiving

My soul is a single dance
with my love, Daniel,
together we waited
for our moment in time

In quietness my soul shines

My soul is a single boy
on a dusty road
in a place no soul would dare to be found

He searches for grains of food
to feed his family and
prays for rain and mercy

My soul is a single pearl

My soul is a single man
Who lived a simple life in an insignificant place
He taught life lessons to those at His side
He walked one road
to one hill
and gave His life
that we might live

My soul is a single note
in a song
written for a single love
that will last a lifetime

My soul is a single poem

My soul is a single hand that reaches
a homeless man
to give a blanket and provide warmth
where none can be found

My soul is a people in a city
set on a hill
who cannot hide their Light
because they are the light
they are a single shout in the earth

I have one prayer
in this one room
with one burning candle
It is that He would touch our hearts
and that we would not take one soul
for granted
ever

In one room
with one candle
that burns in the dark
my soul becomes one prayer
that only one Savior can understand
In that moment
I am at once transformed into
His song, His poem,
His pearl and His praise

Tonight my soul is a psalm of the Lord

Riverbank Redemption

The days become the nights
The nights are works of glory
The crossing of this Jordan
Is my journey and my story

I wade to reach Your holiness
To rest upon the shore
To sit in sands of sanctity
And learn to love You more

How can I attain my place in You
That leaves my cares behind?
Where Spirit flows with Spirit deep
In a soul dance through my mind

I want to know Your thoughts
When I seek Your face in prayer
I want to kiss Your feet my King
And find Your lasting favor

In seas, on shores, on riverbanks
Your Spirit speaks to me
In dawn and dusk and moonlit nights
I glimpse infinity

When I have crossed this river place
This Jordan You ordained
I'll see my dreams redeem the years
You'll give me my new name

I'll study doubt and fear no more
For Your promises are true
My faith will heal your maidens' hearts
To be transformed in You.

Milkshakes and Blues Alley
(@ Mariette)

Girls
friends
girlfriends
unbroken, the circle never ends
God and time is always good to us
even when we don't realize it

We can sit on the porch, drink lemonade and tea
and try to run the world because we know we are qualified
if they would listen to us
we would tell them Who is really running things

Should our prayers for each other be heard in heaven they
would ask for
strong men, children
and enough days to see the goodness of both

I will always remember
the milkshakes, Blues Alley, laughter
and shopping for shoes
I can't forget late night prayers, faith,
interceding for one another and the joy of
worshipping the God that never leaves
never sleeps, always comforts, and always answers
the right prayers right on time

Of all the things I shall always do
I shall always remember you.

Mother River

I am the river in you my children
      of a continent afar off called Dark.
You see, now I know both sides
of the story. I saw it from the beginning, when the
Euphrates
was your water fountain
in that Garden
when you first knew your Name;
there no one could deny you drink.
      Remember
You called to me and I whispered
back: beautiful.

Let me be your river, like the longest Nile
I will take you back as we journey
      to the rich soil
that has so much to tell us
      of a people long ago
      afar off in distant lands.
they left home and became other languages
      pretending now not to know me
the Mother of their youth.
I laugh at their deception.

I am your river, sons and daughters of Japheth
You lost your identity with me
when you tried to give me yours.
      Can't you see, it wasn't yours to give?
Now I offer you sweet sanctified waters.
Drink from my fountains, soothe your conscience
cool in my streams,
      for they are healing streams
      and I saved them just for you.
I don't want to forget, just forgive and forgive
70 times 7.

I am your river, daughters,
Let my warm dark eyes comfort you in your
blue confusion
        you keep trying to find your place

        I know mine
because I was there from the beginning.
Despite the experiences of
having my babies and my men torn from
me I have comfort for you as well.
I already prepared the way for you with cries
that screamed for legitimacy
        and pain encountered without justification
For you I have fresh flora to plant by your
        waterside.

As Deborah, I prophesied victory and ruled a mighty
nation
I know my place
My daughter Jael fought with wisdom,
and by slaying one
saved many.

So place your hands in the thickness of my
hair the braided brooks
there you will find nourishment.
Then come if you will and jump the
double-dutch songs of my youth. Don't you
know my feet compute mathematical
        formulas every time they skip the rope?

I am your river
        Men of darkness and depth
You keep forgetting I was
there through every passage;
        Your rejection dawned on my
day too and I never missed
any of your sorrow
Drink from my riverbeds

and renew your strength
then allow me to gently wrap myself around
you
like a river bend that won't
quit

I stay not because I have to, but
I stay so you won't leave
I stay because I know your
purpose even if you don't
Let my river rain
on your wounds
I told the others I am
healing
Now I am yours to drink from
and there is no end to my Source
We were there together
in the first day
we ought to know each other by now.
We have children to harvest
from violent streets and famined lands
They are ours, they belong to us.

I am your river, you nations
who were once mighty
Ignorance of my stamina will never
advance your cause
You will come back   You have to come back
your completeness is void
without me
I am your river for
I carry a Word.

In my night season I am
quiet
yet carefully conceiving
a new birth
A new nation of children

who abhor hate
and seek the knowledge
of truth that will free them from
      the lies
      Color won't matter then
      They have something to say

If you join your river with mine
we can thrust anger aside
and watercolor a portrait
of tranquil springs.

I have a story
to tell.

      Listen

Tell the children to listen

      Listen

Hear waves of laughter
of sisterhood that binds
through the ages

Hear their jubilant songs
and stories of long
ago
we can't afford to forget.

Listen to me
      as I wind carefully down your
      valleys and mountainsides
         and through your urban
            forests, preserving a people
              a Perfected Praise as I go
      Lift up your heads
         I am here and will
      always be here

        I will never leave.
          I can't leave.

I am your mother
I am your river
I am your Mother River

I carry a Word from the Lord.

Southern Comfort

I am color

without apology

living in prisms deep

I cannot change

I am warm and brown

When Creation created me, He created you

I am in you, have been in you

and will always be in you

fresh as that Eden day

I was birthed between the Tigris

and the Euphrates and lately on small islands

I am southern comfort mocha style

Mother of all

I am living color

without any apology I am warm and brown

rich and smooth

my love is good

my soul satisfied

my color is comfort

One Prophetic Word

Close your eyes and lean into Me
says the Lord of Hosts
For in you I have prepared refreshing that will
overtake you like a mighty river

I am your river of peace, prosperity and joy
When you come into Me, into My presence
A banquet of My love, compassion and
forgiveness awaits you

I am your sword and your shield
I am the God of your right hand
Seek Me, even in the midnight hour and
I will give you rest
I will refresh your soul and satisfy
in that which you long

I have shepherded My people into My kingdom
I will shepherd you
For I have waiting for you a harvest of plenty
There is no lack in My Kingdom
For there is no lack in Me

Teach my people, Teach my Daughters virtue
Teach them My holiness and prepare them
For an entrance of a great light
It is pure and uncompromising
Just as I am
For I AM that I AM
The beginning and the end
Your Alpha and Omega
The God of all peace and of all comfort

I will arise and still every enemy of your
spirit and soul
I will quiet those storms and cause you
To ride on the waves of My wealth
For I created the storms
And will likewise still them in your presence
You will see My salvation
You will experience My joy

You will see My favor, goodness and grace

"And when Jesus was in Bethany at the house of Simon the leper, a woman came to him having an alabaster flask of very costly fragrant oil, and she poured it on His head as He sat at the table. But when His disciples saw it, they were indignant saying, "Why this waste? For this fragrant oil might have been sold for much and given to the poor."

But when Jesus was aware of it, He said to them, "Why do you trouble the woman? For she has done a good work for Me. For you have the poor with you always, but Me you do not have always. For in pouring the fragrant oil on My body, she did it for My burial. Assuredly, I say to you, wherever this gospel is preached in the whole world, what this woman has done will also be told as a memorial to her."

Matthew 26:6-13

Your Road to the Relationship

After reading the pages of this book, you will know that my love for God is intricately woven in the fabric of what I write. My relationship with Christ is at the core of my essence. It is, when all is said and done, everything I have. So that you may walk in the fullness of His love and grace and all that He has, I invite you into that same relationship. With it comes forgiveness for your past, grace to live for today, and a future life with Him in eternity. Praying this simple prayer seals you in Christ and your name is written in the Lamb's Book of Life:

Lord Jesus, come into my life. I accept You as my personal Lord and Savior. I give my life to You and make You the head of my life. I believe in my heart and confess with my mouth that You are the Son of God who came to earth, died for my sins and arose from the dead. I repent of all my sins and ask Your forgiveness. I thank You for Your blood on Calvary that was shed as atonement for my sins. Holy Spirit, come into my life and fill me with your precious Spirit. Activate the gifts in my life and lead me in the places You have ordained for my life.

Now, it's up to you to read your Bible and join a local church that teaches the full Gospel of Jesus Christ. Pray that the Holy Spirit lead you to a pastor who is after the heart of God, who will teach you to walk in His word, and use your gifts for the advancement of the Kingdom of God.

I hope that with each turn of the page you were drawn in and captivated by the words and thoughts of my heart. I can't wait to pen another tapestry of words.

Until we meet again,

Melanie L Houston

About the Author

Melanie Houston is the founder and chief executive officer of Alabaster Box Media Group, a division of Vision Resources, Inc. Alabaster Box Media Group is a company dedicated to publishing, producing, and promoting literary works that advance the Gospel of Jesus Christ. Melanie also serves as the chief operations officer of Daniel Houston & Associates, a provider of management consulting, training and executive coaching services.

Melanie's professional background includes human resource and management experience that exceeds 30 years in corporate America and with her own consulting firm. Clients include national and international profit and nonprofit organizations in the areas of community service, publishing, energy, telecommunications, microelectronics and chambers of commerce. She has served as an executive editor for an award-winning national publishing house, an international magazine, and several independent publishers.

A native of Columbus, Ohio, Melanie is a graduate of Capital University with a Bachelor of Arts degree in art therapy. She received a Master of Arts degree from The Ohio State University, with a major in labor and human resource management.

In her spare time, she enjoys creating works of art, jewelry design, and reading a good book. She celebrates the covenant of marriage with Daniel A. Houston, chief executive officer of The 1750 Group, Inc./Daniel Houston & Associates.

Visit her at www.alabasterboxmedia.com

ALABASTER BOX
MEDIA GROUP